CUSTOMIZING VANS

Mitch Beedie

CUSTOMIZING
VANS

ARCO N.Y.

Published by Arco Publishing Company, Inc.,
219 Park Avenue South, New York, N.Y. 10003.

Copyright © 1978 by Blaketon Hall Limited

Printed in Great Britain

Library of Congress Cataloging in Publication Data

Beedie, Mitch

Customizing Vans

1. Vans–Customizing   I.   Title

TL298.B39 1978   629.28'8'6   78-4500

ISBN 0-668-04542-6

Contents

Choosing a Van   10

Bodywork Repairs
and Painting   14

Spray Painting Basics   20

Murals   26

Portholes and
Skylights   32

Lettering   38

Glass Etching   40

Interiors   41

Show Vans   49

More Custom
Goodies   63

Appendix   81

Choosing a Van

For a van that will give you many years of trouble-free service; one that is not going to leak and rattle, or be time-consuming and expensive to repair, you should buy from a franchised dealer. On top of the price of the vehicle itself, consider the following extras:

★ portholes, a skylight, and a raised top

★ the interior of the van (beds, cooker, fridge, stereo, T.V., cupboards, sink unit, toilet, carpets, insulation, panelling)

★ paint − a complete respray, custom painting on the panels, or both

★ roof-rack

★ extra lights

★ captain's chairs

★ wide wheels, spoilers for front and rear, and wheel flares

You might not want all of these things, so list your needs. If you do the work yourself, it will cost less than if you give it to a professional, but there are some jobs you may not want to tackle. The type and size of van you choose and the extras you pick will depend upon the intended use of the vehicle.

Whatever your choice, you must get a van with a big enough payload. When vanning, passengers, fuel, cooker, fridge, beds, sink and luggage all have to be carried. To find the payload, subtract the kerb weight of the van from its GVW (Gross Vehicle Weight).

The Ford Transit particularly, available in many options, has a lot to offer the customizer, and it has a well-deserved reputation for reliability. The power plant can be diesel or gasoline; it has good suspension; drives well and can be manoeuvred as easily as a car.

New or used?

After budgeting for van and accessories, your choice may be between a new van and one that has been carefully used. A new van will obviously cost more initially, and may depreciate in the first year. On the other hand, you can order a new semi-custom model with basic needs; carpeted and with special seats, and your additions will certainly increase its value. An old van will be less comfortable than a new one and will cost slightly more to run, as it will probably need more servicing and spare parts. Many buyers have found that a good compromise is to buy a one-year old uncustomized van, which will already have depreciated and is, therefore, relatively inexpensive.

Choose a model with power to spare. The van should have a payload of at least ¾-ton, and preferably more. Heavy-duty springs and shock-absorbers are also essential, and get the largest radiator, battery and alternator available, and a high-output heater. Power steering and brakes and a fast rear axle ratio make for comfortable long-distance driving. A van option with the fewest windows will be cheaper than a model with windows already installed. You may want to fit portholes anyway, and the inside of the van is tricky to panel if there are windows already there.

TRANS AMERICAN VAN

Automotive stylist Harry Bradley designed this low and sleek, highly modified, vehicle for Bob Larivee—6-ins. was removed from the suspension and another 6-ins. from the lower body, resulting in a custom vehicle some 12-ins. lower than the ex-works van, yet retaining full visibility. Other modifications included moving the rear axle and substituting heavy-duty front springs. The interior sports racing style seats and steering wheel, and a carpeted floor, with brushed metal side panels.

Raised roof at the rear gives good interior height and darkened windows provide forward vision whilst retaining privacy.

Buying a new van with air-conditioning, tinted windows, stereo and so on, will save you the trouble of doing the work yourself, but it will be more expensive and you will miss out on the fun of doing it yourself. If you go half way and buy a part-customized cruising van, to which you can add your personal requirements, this will get you well on the way and provide a fun vehicle that can be used at once and gradually improved as funds permit.

Bodywork Repairs
and
Painting

How to:

★ remove dents and deal with body damage

★ add wide wheels, wheel flares and spoilers

★ prepare surface for painting

★ paint your van

★ produce special effects: murals, signs, etc.

The preparatory tools required are:

★ fine and coarse emery cloth

★ sponge, plus hose or bucket

★ sanding block (an electric sander will do the job faster than a hand one)

★ 'cheese-grater' file

★ zinc gauze

Before starting work, read through the techniques and decide how much you can do yourself, and what to leave for a professional. Time and patience, plus a basic skill with tools, are needed for a first-class job.

Removing dents and body damage

A professional body finisher can pinpoint dents by touch alone. A slower (but just as effective) method is to take a flat surfaced block, wrap fine-grade emery cloth round it, and sand down the paintwork, using a hose or wet sponge to keep the surface wet. Paint will be taken off the high spots, while the low spots will stay shiny. If any paint chips off while you are sanding, it indicates that the top layer or layers are badly bonded to those below. Small areas are nothing to worry about, and they are easily dealt with. They could be the result of bad paint bonding over an earlier repair. Sand down all these areas until a stable layer of underlying paint is exposed.

After sanding, take a felt tipped pen and ring areas that need attention. There will be four main categories:

★ low spots deeper than ¼-in.

★ badly dented high spots, i.e. dents from inside the van

★ less serious low spots (which can be filled with filler)

★ less serious high spots

To fill the low spots, clean the surface thoroughly and roughen it so that the filler will adhere. Mix the filler as instructed by the maker, and work it carefully into the dents. There should be no air bubbles in the finished work. Apply the filler to extend well beyond the damaged area. When the filler has set, but before it has fully hardened, use a grater file to shave off most of the excess. After the filler hardens, use coarse emery cloth around a block to sand again. Finally, sand with fine emery cloth and a hose to achieve a smooth surface. If you need to re-apply filler at any time, first roughen the surface with coarse emery cloth to improve adhesion.

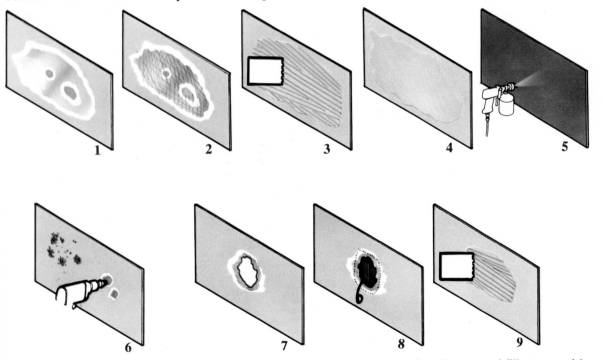

1. Sand damaged area to expose low spots.
2. Score sanded area to provide a key.
3. Spread filler over area.
4. Sand down until smooth.
5. Spray with primer, allow to dry, then sand until smooth.
6. Clean rust spots with wire brush, and repeat steps 3-5.
7. For holes, clean rust to expose clean metal.
8. Put ring of filler around inside of hole, insert piece of zinc gauze behind hole and pull forward with wire.
9. When filler has set, remove wire handle and fill hole. Pro-Proceed as in steps 4 & 5.

Wide Wheels, Wheel Flares and Spoilers.

The installation of wide wheels is an expensive job, but well worth the cost. Springs and shackles may need alteration to raise the body, so that the wheel arch has the necessary clearance, and the new wheels will have to be balanced after fitting. Only keen and skilled mechanics should undertake this operation: your van dealer will gladly do the job for you.

Bolt-on flares

1. Clamp wheel flare in position.

2. Mark ill-fitting spots for grinding.

3. Reclamp after grinding and drill for bolts.

4. Use washers both sides plus a spring washer under nut.

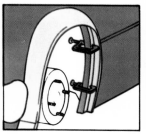  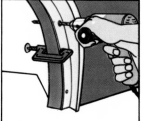 

If you add wide wheels, you will need wheel flares to comply with the law. Spoilers are usually added at the same time, as they can be blended with the flares for a smoother appearance. They serve to reduce air turbulence under the van. The easiest way to add these extras is to buy a kit: several types are advertised in custom-car magazines. Flares and spoilers straight out of a kit will almost certainly leave unsightly gaps between them and the bodywork, so it is wise to first use G-clamps to fix the front spoilers into position, and follow them by the two front side flares. Mark those areas that do not fit snugly, and trim off excess as required. Fibreglass cuts easily, so cut a piece off, check by reclamping, cut another piece off, and so on. Once the components fit to your satisfaction, leave them clamped in place while you drill the mounting holes as close to the outer surface of the flare as possible. Make sure that the holes, where the ends of the spoiler meet the flares, are in exact alignment, so that flares and spoiler join smoothly. When you bolt them together, use a flat washer and a lock-washer under each nut. The rear flares and wheel arches can be similarly fitted.

Moulded flares are more durable than 'bolt-ons', but are more difficult to fit. Do not be tempted to mould 'bolt-on' flares to the van with filler without bolts, as the joint will eventually crack. Remember that even slight ripples in the filler will show when the van is finally painted, so care should be taken to ensure perfect smoothness.

Bolt-on fibreglass flares bonded to body

1. Clean area beneath flare to bright metal and coat with epoxy resin.	2. Bolt on flare, coat with resin and lay glass cloth over joint.	3. Grind down glass cloth and coat with filler.	4. Sand down to a smooth finish and coat with primer.

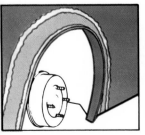
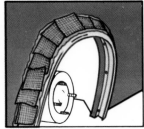
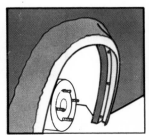
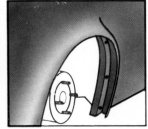

DUSTY ROSE — highly lac-
quered gloss finish of envious
quality and an interior to
match—vantastic!

Another view of DUSTY
ROSE showing the side door
and the slotted wheel design
chosen.

Seen from behind, this custom trailer looks like a van, and has almost the same load capacity as its towing vehicle.

A matching trailer is a great way to carry additional gear and keeps the van interior free from clutter. Trailers can have fixed cookers and gas and water storage facilities.

Spray Painting Basics

Spray guns

When spraying one van it is best to hire a compatible gun and compressor. When hiring, explain the type of paint you will be using and the nature of the job, and ask for the most suitable gun and compressor. For cellulose enamel paint you can use a standard compressor and spray gun with a No. 1 nozzle.

Types of paint

Acrylic enamel is a slow-drying paint. If the surface is scratched within a week of the body being painted, you cannot spray over the scratch without lifting the original layer. A surface that has been painted with acrylic enamel takes eight months to fully harden: special hardeners are available that cut drying time down to a day. These are expensive, and require the van to be kept in a dust-free atmosphere for four hours, as compared to one hour for normal acrylic enamel, but they improve final gloss, and increase the life expectancy of the surface by up to 50 per cent.

Acrylic lacquer is the fastest drying paint; dust-resistant after half an hour, and favoured by custom painters. It must be sprayed on in light coats for maximum gloss, and about five or six coats are required.

Cellulose enamel is another fast-drying paint, which resists dust after one and a half hours, and you can respray scratches without lifting the original surface.

DENIM BLUE — an ideal delivery van for a denim manufacturer.

Both acrylic and cellulose enamel are diluted with 'reducers', whereas acrylic lacquer is diluted with 'thinners'. Manufacturers provide ratios of thinner to paint which must be observed. Use the correct primer before you paint a surface. The best primers are those based on zinc chromate or zinc tetroxy-chromate. Do not use a lead-based primer. You must consult the manufacturer, as the primer has to be formulated especially for the paint you are using.

Vans with acrylic or cellulose enamel paintwork must be primed and painted with acrylic cellulose or enamel. If you want to use an acrylic lacquer custom finish, you must cover the existing paint-work with several coats of sealer first. You can test the paint on your van by spraying a small unimportant corner with acrylic lacquer. If the original paint lifts off or bubbles it is enamel.

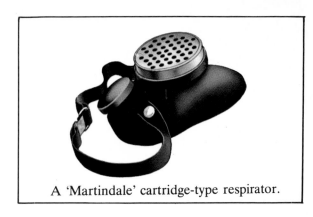

A 'Martindale' cartridge-type respirator.

When painting, use a cartridge-type respirator, and change the cartridge each time you use the gun. If you have no respirator, then do not paint. Besides being toxic, paint is highly inflammable, and there should be no naked lights or sparks around when you paint.

Painting

Tape around the rain gutter, and erect some scaffolding so that you can easily reach the roof. Wet down the floor to settle any dust, and ground the van with a chain to kill static and prevent it from attracting dust. Clean the van with a non-caustic, non-powdered cleanser—washing-up liquid will do if you cannot get the proper cleanser. When perfectly dry, spray three or four light coats of paint onto the roof (if you are using acrylic lacquer, then seal the original paint surface, and spray five coats of lacquer). Allow sufficient drying time after each coat to avoid runs. Work from the centre of the roof out towards the sides. As soon as you have finished the last coat, clean your spray gun and leave the area immediately, so that you don't raise unnecessary dust.

Come back to the van after a day, and mask your newly-painted roof. For a two-tone effect, paint the top half of the van first, mask if off, and then paint the bottom half. Clean the sides of the van before painting, and when spraying, be extra careful not to cause any sags or runs. Use smooth, overlapping, horizontal passes, each no more than 2–4 ft. long. Keep the gun at right-angles to the side of the van, and always about 2 ft. away from it. Spray three or four coats (unless you are using acrylic lacquer, when you should spray on at least five coats), and again leave the area as soon as you have finished.

Remove the masking tape after two to three hours, when the paint is no longer sticky, but is not hard. Tape removed too soon may peel the paint off with it, but if removed too late the paint may chip off at the edges.

If you are not going to add a custom paint finish, it is best to seal the paint with a clear sealer, which can be waxed and polished when dry.

An American van with a complex pattern of carefully blended shades of mauve.

Stars and stripes of a different kind created with the aid of paper masks.

 1.

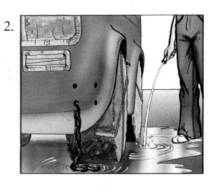 2.

 3.

 4.

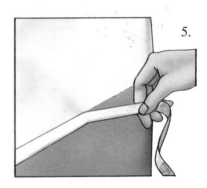 5.

1. Remove brightwork and carefully mask areas not to be painted.

2. Earth the body to avoid static and damp the floor to lay dust.

3. Start with the roof; the body sides masked.

4. Go on to the top half of the sides and then the bottom half.

5. Use masking tape and paper (not shown) for a clean line.

Paintwork after-care is important! Wash with plenty of water to remove grime before drying and polishing.

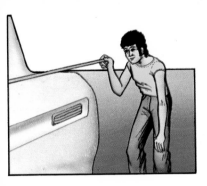

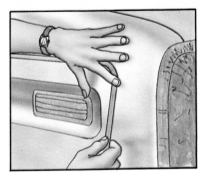

1. Sighting along tape to get a straight line. When perfectly straight allow to touch body.

2. Mask carefully for natural curves in custom stripes. Ensure tape sticks perfectly to avoid paint creeping underneath it.

3. Use brown paper and tape, and mask areas from overspray.

4. Sand mural area to a matt finish to accept further paint coats and give good adhesion.

Variations on a theme. Custom stripes 'n zig-zags transform fairly basic vans into excitingly different paint jobs.

Murals

A full-scale mural is a big undertaking, and unless you are artistic, and have a good knowledge of the mediums and techniques that you will be using, plus plenty of time, they can easily go wrong. A professional custom painter will often spray thirty or more coats on a panel to gradually build up a mural; the finished job depending to a large extent upon the sprayer's skill in blending the colours that cover each other. If you think you have the ability, have a go. At worst, you can sand off and start again!

The surface should be prepared as for panel painting:

★ simple designs can be sprayed through paper masks, or masks made from special tacky adhesive material used for airbrush masking and available at art stores. Paper masks can be taped in position, but they must be close-fitting. Airbrush masking material is expensive but worth it as it overcomes potential problems of seepage.

★ a spray gun can be used for general background, an airbrush for finer work, and a lettering brush for very fine detail.

★ basic shapes can be added with a dark paint; they will still show through even when covered with lighter tints.

★ know when to stop! There comes a point where adding more coats makes the mural look worse, not better.

Aerosols, available in great variety, can be used for murals. Those with large nozzles can be used instead of a spray gun, and the fine nozzle variety can be used instead of an airbrush.

A cheaper and less time-consuming way to put a mural on your van is to buy one and stick it on. Excellent murals are advertised in magazines, but since the finished job is not unique, it is therefore less satisfying than a personally executed, individual design.

A 'soft' airbrush technique that has worked well.

This type of modern art is becoming highly collectible. On vans it looks great and draws attention wherever it goes.

1. A pre-cut stencil used as a mask.

2. Many varied effects can be obtained.

3. Sand area of mural to a matt finish and remove dust.

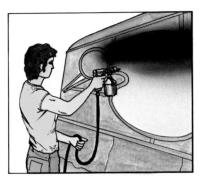

4. Spray carefully, covering in passes from left to right, right to left.

5. Using an airbrush for the basic outline.

6. Nearing completion. Detail can be added with fine art brushes.

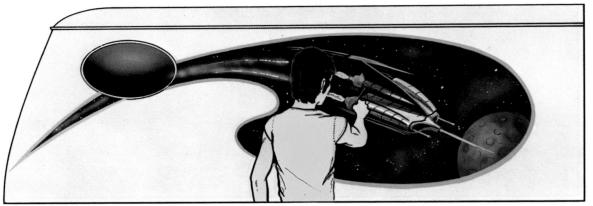

Mural techniques of endless variety ...

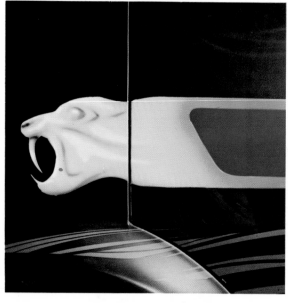

 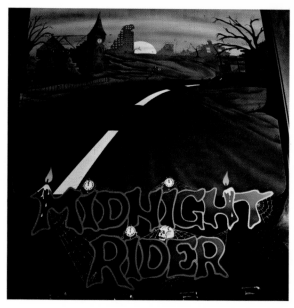

MIDNIGHT RIDER
Two varying styles on the same vehicle, lend interest and excitement.

LONDON SCENE — a well executed, tasteful paint job.

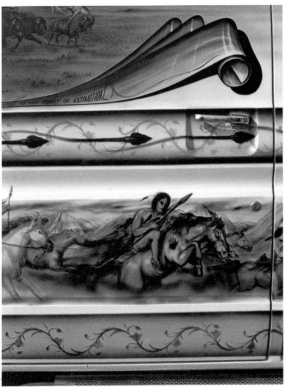

Mural art shown on American
vans. Time, patience and skill
are all essential to produce
results like these.

Portholes and Skylights

The tools you will need are:

★ sabre saw

★ drill

★ scriber

★ power chisel or hacksaw

★ flexible sealant

★ ¼-in. plywood board

★ screwdriver

★ square-edge

★ masking tape and paper

★ wrench

★ heavy-duty
plastic hammer

Sunlight, fresh air, and space to move around in will help you to feel at home in your van. Portholes let in sunlight; skylights can let in the sun and also ventilate the van. A raised top enables you to stand up on the rare occasions that you need to, but also provides a feeling of having lots more space—have a look inside a van with one installed, and you'll see what I mean. They are best installed by a professional who has the experience to overcome the difficulties encountered in making them leakproof.

Installing a skylight

Besides looking attractive and letting in the sun, a skylight adds to the efficiency of your van's ventilation. When you are moving, air is drawn through the van's system, and is expelled through the hatch of the skylight. Install your skylight above the cooker and it will take away cooking smells.

There are basically two types of skylight; one has an outer frame that screws into the top of the roof, and an inner frame that screws into the head-liner. With the other type, the top frame fits into the roof, and the lower frame screws into the top frame. Whichever type of frame you have, remember to balance the stresses when fitting. Skylights can be either square or oblong; different makers use different ways of opening and closing the hatch, but installation is basically the same for all of them. Install the skylight on a flat surface in your van's roof (remembering to put a blanket on the roof if you clamber over it). Twelve inches from the rear should be about right, or further forward if you want to reserve the rear for a roof rack or a raised top. It is possible to obtain contoured frames if you are putting the skylight in a small van. Make a template from the skylight, place the template on the roof of the van, and centre it accurately. Mark the roof and make a starter hole inside the marked area. Use a sabre-saw to cut 1½-ins. inside the template mark, to leave a lip. Make sure that the hinge of the skylight faces to the front of the van, so that air can flow over the hatch: if the hinge is at the back, or even at the side, then the force of the headwind when you are travelling may rip the hatch off. Make a series of small cuts at each corner and bend the lip back inside the van, then check that the skylight fits properly.

Pull out any insulation, and cut a hole in the head-liner panel to correspond with that in the roof. This hole shoud be an inch or so smaller all round than that in the van roof; you can trim the excess material off later. If there is a rib on the head-liner panel itself, cut it back so that the inner surround frame will fit up against the roof. Replace the head-liner panel, and put wood spacers between the panel and the roof, as before. Seal around the top of the opening with flexible sealant and lower the skylight into place (with the hinge facing the front of the van). Remember that any gaps you leave now will leak later, so check that you can see no daylight through the join between the roof and the skylight. Screw the skylight into position, and trim off the excess material and cut away the surplus sealant for a professional finish.

Tall portholes or windows may pull the van wall out of shape (portholes are flat, van walls curve), so keep to the flat area of the wall. Often you will find that the best place in the wall to put your porthole is just across one of the van ribs. If so, you have two choices: reposition the porthole in between two ribs, or cut away part of the offending rib. If you decide to cut away the rib, use a power chisel or hacksaw to make one cut just below the van's beltline, and the other just below the roof. Weaken the spot-welds by drilling them with a $^3/_{16}$ to $^3/_4$-in. bit. Now work the rib to and fro until the spot-welds break (if you cannot budge the rib, use a heavy-duty plastic hammer to hammer it out, but be careful or you will damage the panel). The porthole that you will be fitting will supply some of the rigidity that the rib gave, but the wall will be weakened to some extent.

Existing rear windows can be replaced by special shapes or new windows inserted into plain doors.

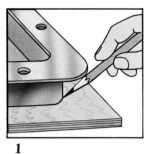 1

 2

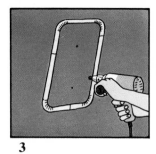 3

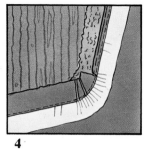 4

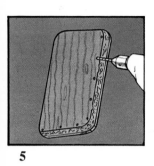 5

 6

 7

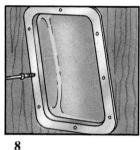 8

Fitting windows and portholes

1. Trace outline of window frame onto plywood and cut out.

2. Screw plywood template in position and scribe shape onto van side.

3. Stick masking tape on outside of scribed line, remove template, drill ¾-in. hole, ¾-in. inside line for saw-blade starting point.

4. Using sabre saw, cut out window shape ¾-in. *inside* scribed line, remove any insulation and bend edges back to form a strengthened lip.

5. From outside van, drill small holes through inner panelling to mark edges of hole.

6. Replace template inside van using holes as a guide. Scribe outline.

7. Drill hole for saw-blade ¾-in. inside scribed line. Cut out. Fit wooden spacers about ½-in. apart, (for clarity, illus. shows fewer spacers).

8. Fit window frame and its bezel and screw together, tightening screws in diagonal sequence.

Portholes are available in a wide variety of shapes and sizes. The technique of fitting is similar for all.

This beautiful van sports a
design that is highly complex,
yet appears deceptively simple.
A fine example of the
customizer's art.

Lettering

Lettering with diffraction tape

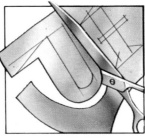

1. Trace lettering onto tape.

2. Cut out letters.

3. Stick to van side.

4. Use a brush to add outline if required.

HAVOC

Silver pearl over white paintwork with patterns in Aztec Gold candy, cobwebbing in Aubergine with black shaddowing and Royal Blue candy lettering...pure havoc!

HOT'N BOTHERED

A very good example of lettering with diffraction tape—tastefully executed.

BLACK GOLD — good example of paint work using silhouette techniques through paper masks.

Lettering: from the simple to the exotic.

Applying decals

Although decals are not unique, when carefully applied they can be extremely attractive.

1. Tape decal to van side, remove backing sheet from one half of decal.

2. Cut away half of backing sheet.

3. Smooth down half of the decal onto van, expelling all air bubbles.

4. Repeat proceedure for other half, then remove protective covering from front.

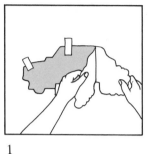
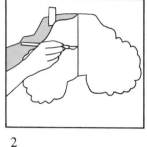

1   2   3   4

Etching window glass

1. Cover design area of window with adhesive transparent material bought at an art supplies store. Mask surrounding area with several thicknesses of paper.

2. Trace design onto tape. Simple designs work better.

3. Cut out design from tape and peel away from areas to be blasted.

4. Wear protective clothing, an anorak, gloves and goggles will do.

5. A permanent card stencil can be cut for repetitive designs.

6. With experience, vignetted designs can be achieved using similar technique to airbrushing.

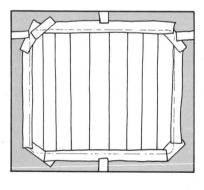
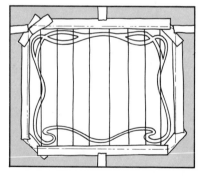
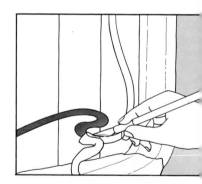

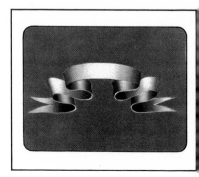

Interiors

Artist's impression of a comfortable week-ender with no cooking, washing or other facilities.

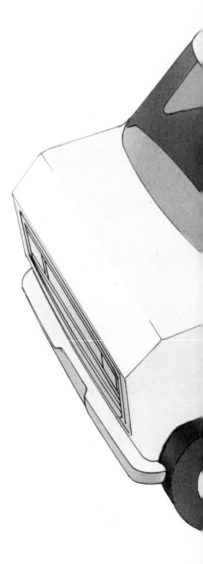

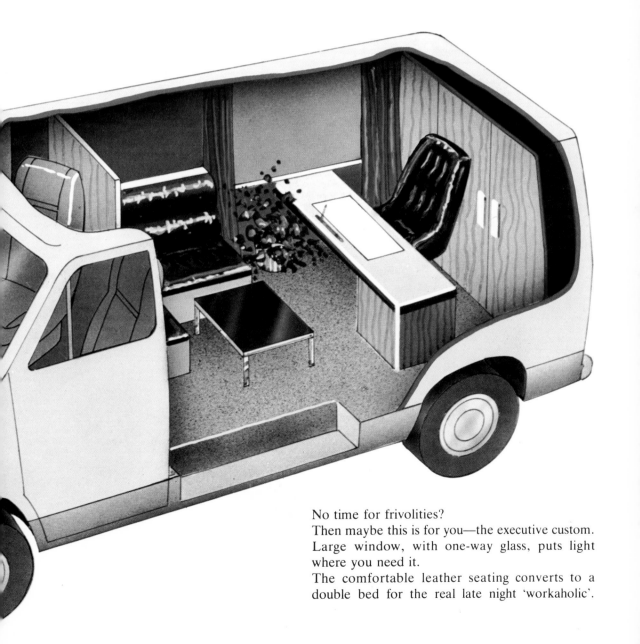

No time for frivolities?
Then maybe this is for you—the executive custom.
Large window, with one-way glass, puts light
where you need it.
The comfortable leather seating converts to a
double bed for the real late night 'workaholic'.

Insulation and panelling

The installation of panelling, insulation, and a van floor, is similar whether your van is to become a motor caravan, a custom-van, or for goods carrying. The difference is in the degree of insulation you will need, the type of finish the interior will have, and whether or not there will be cut-outs in the panelling for equipment to be installed.

Depending upon the type of van you have bought, the interior may be bare metal (if you have a commercial van), or it may already have wall and roof panels.

The floor

Remove everything from the interior of the van—brackets, spare wheel, sun visors, door handles, and the head-liner panel should all come out. Vacuum the floor of the van thoroughly and treat with a rustproofing compound.

Run suitable cables for light points, speakers, extra battery and other equipment. Leave plenty of cable at each end so that you have no problems when you come to connect to it. Tape the speaker wires, and the cable for the extra battery, to the valleys in the floor.

Chip-board or particle-board is good for floor covering; it cuts easily, but is not as strong or as flexible as plywood, and becomes weaker when wet. A single plywood sheet may suffice to cover the floor, but this material should be treated to avoid warping. Both chip-board and plywood can be easily covered by rubber-backed lino or heavy-duty carpet. Treated plywood covered with heavy-duty rubber sheet is used in many buses and coaches. It is durable, provides good insulation, and is available in many different colours and thicknesses.

The floor should be fitted before the wall panels, so that any condensation that forms between the panelling and the van wall, will run down the inside of the metal wall of the van, onto the wooden floor, rather than under it. Condensation that collects in this way is a nuisance, but harmless. Place the floor covering board so that it fits right up to the sides. Measure the parts of the panel which need cut-outs (around the rear wheel-wells, side door, and, if the van has no side-panelling, the van ribs). Allow ½-in. clearance for the wheel-wells, and as much as is necessary around the side door (make a paper template to show how much should be cut away so that the door does not catch the floor). Screw the panel to the floor with 1½-in. sheet-metal screws, 8-ins. apart, avoiding the valleys.

If the wood floor is being covered with lino, its surface must be smooth—any bumps or screw heads will show through. Sand down the wood, countersink the screws, and fill the holes with wood putty. Lino should not be glued down immediately after you unroll it, as it tends to 'creep' for a few days. For carpet, screw long strips of 2-ins. wide, ⅝-in. thick wood around the edges of the floor to which the carpet can be fixed. Instead of thin

Adding floor and padding

1. Clean floor and paint with rust inhibiting paint.

2. Cut and screw down ply or chip-board panels; avoid placing screws in valleys.

3. Lay foam underlay, the heavy type will need no adhesive.

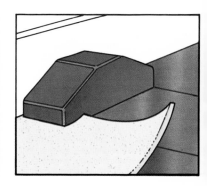

underlay, thick padding can be used, made from 2-ins. thick firm-grade sponge foam. To stick the padding to the wooden floor, apply a generous coat of strong glue to the padding and another to the floor; let the glue become tacky, and press the padding into place. Padding should be oversize and trimmed when the glue has dried. Where carpet comes up to the side and rear doors, it can either be stapled to the vertical edge of those long strips of wood that hold the carpet in place, or you can use metal trim strip, into which the edge of the carpet is fitted. This provides a neat edge, from which the carpet can easily be released if required.

Insulate the rear wheel arches and glue pieces of rug over them. If the wheel-wells will be visible, make a good job of this, with a rectangular piece of rug sewn to a semi-circular piece. Sew them together with a heavy-duty sewing machine with the wrong sides facing out: a sail-maker will often help you out. Turn the cover the right way out, and glue it carefully to the wheel-well. The bottom of the rug can be tucked into the space left between the wheel-well and floor panels.

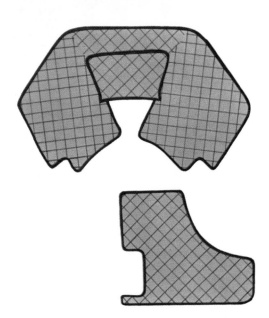

Quilted covers can be purchased or made from material bought by the yard. Ideal for covering engine humps in the cab.

Carpet fitting

1. Fit wooden battens around all edges, using self-tapping screws. Alternatively, use proprietary carpet gripper.

2. Cut and fit carpet, and staple to battens.

3. Shape to fit around wheel arches.

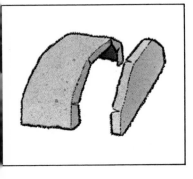

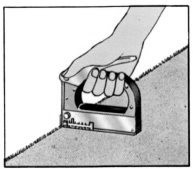

4. Cut pieces to cover wheel arches and stitch together.

5. Glue in position.

6. Tuck edges under main carpet.

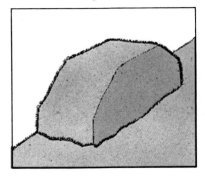

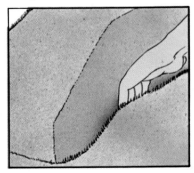

Insulation

The choice of insulation will depend upon weather conditions. The cheapest way to buy insulation is to purchase remnants—10 or 12-in. scrap pieces will be the best. Trim the pieces and fit them between the van ribs, using strong glue (the same glue you used for the floor).

Fibreglass backed with foil can be used to insulate vans. Some people won't use it because fibreglass particles can break loose and get inside the van, where they can cause irritation if they come in contact with the skin. If you do use fibreglass, to avoid irritation when fitting it, wear gloves.

Whatever material you use should be flameproof, should deaden sound, and be easy to fit. An insulating material made from fire-proofed foam fulfills these conditions, and is worth enquiring about. Finally, if you want to go the whole way, you can spray the van walls with a polyurethane foam. It is sprayed on as a liquid and expands to a semi-rigid foam within a few minutes. The foam is impregnated with millions of small bubbles, to insulate and sound-proof the van. You must use a special gun and a cartridge-type respirator when spraying, and oil any surfaces that you do not want covered. Foam is extremely difficult to remove from a surface unless you have previously oiled it. The whole of the cab can be masked off with a single sheet of polythene.

Insulation and panelling

1. Glue pieces of insulation material between box section ribs, wear protective gloves.

2. After fixing insulation, cut roof panel and use padded support stick. Check that panel is centrally positioned.

3. Screw in place. Space screws no more than 8-ins. apart, use self-tapping screws in prepared holes.

4. Where floor ribs are of uneven height or where preferred, wood stringers or cleats can be fixed and the floor screwed to them.

5. When screwing side panels, work lowest screws first and progress towards top to avoid warping problems.

6. Plastic T section can be used for a neat join between panels.

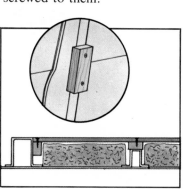

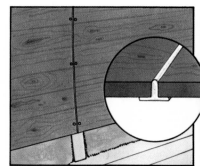

Panelling

For the ceiling and wall panels you can either do everything yourself, including measuring up and making the templates; you can buy a set of plans for your particular van and do the rest yourself; you can buy a kit for your van; or you can get a professional to do the work.

The do-it-yourself man will find an electric drill, and an electric screwdriver a great time saver, as the panelling will require a few hundred screw holes to be drilled.

For the panelling a particle-board covered with fabric looks good, and insulates the van against noise. It is not as durable as plywood, and does not curve easily to fit the van walls.

Formica backed with plywood is durable and very easy to clean. Three-ply sheets are most suited to the parts that need to stand up to heavy use (around the sides of the van), two-ply sheets are best for the ceiling, where the van curves more as it comes down to meet the walls. Some customizers use wooden frames that fix to the metal ribs on the ceiling and walls of the van. The plywood is then screwed to the wooden frame and does not have to bend as much as if it were fitted to the metal ribs. This is only really necessary if you are using three-ply sheets to cover the whole of the interior—ceiling as well as walls. Two-ply sheets should bend sufficiently to be fitted directly to the metal ribs.

If you want the cab to match the rest of the van's colour scheme, you will have to do something with the head-liner panel. This panel is fixed to a metal lip about the windscreen, so you can take it down and replace it with one of your panels, which you can screw into place. This is an exacting job, and the new head-liner panel must be precisely cut to fit properly.

To fit the ceiling, position an 8 ft. x 4 ft. sheet of panelling so that it stretches from the rear of the head-liner panel back along the ceiling of the van. This panel must be centralised, so check side-to-side alignment while it is held in place by a padded support stick. Use another sheet of panelling to cover the rear part of the ceiling.

The interior of DUSTY ROSE

If you use three-ply sheets for the walls, or if you want the ease of working with two-ply, you can fit wooden slats between the metal ribs on either side of the van, which will serve as a wooden frame and will prevent the panels from rippling.

Make templates for the rear wheel arches and use them to mark the side panels. Accuracy is essential when making cut-outs for the wheel arches, so measure carefully. Screw the panels to the walls, or blocks if you have fitted them. Cut two smaller panels to fill the spaces between the main wall panels and the rear doors—fit one either side of the van.

A neat way to fill the spaces between the ceiling and the wall panels is to cut a strip a foam-backed, imprinted vinyl and to secure it with decorative washers and screws.

If you use fabric-covered panelling, the panels will fit together snugly; Formica joins can be made less evident by concealing them with butting pieces: long T-shaped sections, which are glued into the spaces between the panels. The visible part is very thin, and almost unnoticeable.

The joins between the ceiling, walls and the floor can be tidied up with beading.

The front door panels need holes drilled for handles etc., and should be fitted with the windows closed—otherwise you could crack the glass when drilling holes or inserting screws. The stresses should be balanced when you screw the panel in. First put in one screw at the top left-hand corner, then one at the bottom right, and so on. In this way the risk of buckling the panel is reduced.

Remember to cut-out places for the speakers in the back of the van—the cut-outs should be at the same height either side of the doors. Pull the speaker wires through the cut-outs when fitting the panel.

Interior woodwork

1. Typical couch unit built from particle-board and hardboard with a minimum of skilled woodwork required.

2. Doors that open downwards are practical.

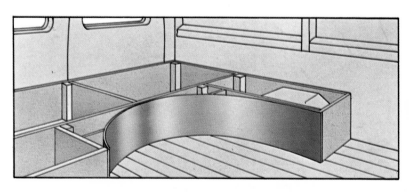

3. Wooden blocks used to fix framing to wheel wells, simple yet solid.

4. Metal brackets can be used to fix framing to floors and walls.

5. Part of a simple divider panel, cut in two halves. Each half may vary, so cut separately.

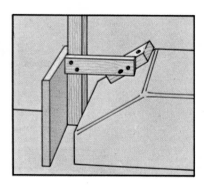

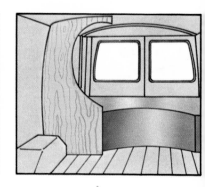

Show Vans

It is quite possible that you want the van to be a showpiece, and that you will not be living in it for any length of time. If so, you will not be satisfied with simple panelling on the walls. The fashion for putting thick-pile carpet all over the inside of the van is tending to die out. Unless the job is done very well, the van tends to look rather overdone and can be a bit like a coffin. However, when tastefully done, and with the right choice of short pile materials, it can look stunning.

A raised platform over part of the van can provide a couch, bed, and storage space. It is basically a large box made of ⅜-in. chip-board that extends from wall to wall, and from the rear door edge to just in front of the wheel arches.

Captain's chairs plus a swivelling seat behind provides comfortable seating for 3.

A raised platform couch with storage under provides comfort during sleeping or waking hours.

Viewed from the rear, the lush interior of Ford's 'LAWRENCE OF ARABIA'.

The basic platform can be varied in many ways—a multiple-level platform coupled with a double-layered wall-divider makes a cosy private bedroom, especially if you add thick curtains which can be closed to separate it from the rest of the van. Cupboard type doors or drawers in the rear of the platform will give access to tools, sleeping bags, or whatever you decide to store in there. With a semi-circular cut-out in front it can be used as a couch. It can be covered with foam and upholstered, or can simply be carpeted and an airbed used at night.

Drink cabinets are becoming more and more popular in converted vans, but wine is best purchased as required, for the constant movement of the van is not to its advantage.

Large cushions scattered around the van are cheap, easy to make, and are a simple way of adding a touch of luxury. They can match or contrast with your colour scheme, and will provide you with a comfortable lounging area, whose character can quickly be changed.

Art posters add to a van's appearance on the inside, but they should be small and match the mood of the van. Do not have too many, or the small space will look cluttered.

The exterior of this fun-filled van is no less exciting and beautiful.

The overall effect that you create in your van will depend very much on the combination of materials, colour scheme and lighting. The lighting can be varied until just the right mood is obtained. Used car lots are a good place to pick up interior lights, many from expensive models, but at inexpensive prices.

When preparing a van for a show, you first have to decide what extras you are going to install, and you also have to choose a theme. Once you have decided on your theme, stick to it. Anything that sounds like a good idea, but doesn't fit into the general scheme, should be quickly forgotten. An eye for detail is of great importance when converting the van—not too much, nor too little. Summon up all your reserves of skill, imagination, and taste before you start the work, and look round at any other vans you can find. See how they have done the work, what their central concept is, and how well they have carried that concept through.

A good tough carpet and warm wood panelling provide an inviting interior to this van fresh from the custom shop. A few personal items of gear, a TV and some bright cushions will soon provide a 'lived in' feeling.

A cruising van based on the new Ford Transit

The prototype cruising van shown here closely follows the theme of the vans which have proved so popular in the USA. The basic Transit 100 van is customized by the use of metallic strato silver paint covered by a hard lacquer, to preserve its finish and add lustre. The standard black grille and windscreen surround are retained, and black paint is added for effect around the cab door and tailgate windows. Black paint is also added below the bumpers to give them a deeper look, and carried through down the sides of the van at below bumper height to give the effect of greater ground clearance. The black paint is topped with a red and orange stripe and a very thin blue 'discord' line. Side-mounted Thrush exhaust pipes add to the squat appearance of the whole vehicle, and are finished in black chrome to match the black body paintwork.

The standard wheels and tyres are replaced by Wolfrace 6½ x 14-in. alloy wheels, fitted with sixty percent profile Pro-Trac 60 tyres featuring raised white lettering on the side walls. These wheels and tyres fit inside the standard wheel arch and do not therefore have an adverse effect on handling.

Other features which could be fitted are a tinted windscreen, the use of a Fiesta sun roof and the tinted tailgate glass. Interest has been added to the front by the addition of two spotlights and a shallow full-width spoiler.

Customized interior

The van features a space-age styled interior, fitted out by Wolfrace Custom Vehicles of Bedford, but this is only one of thousands of possible designs and was done simply for the sake of completeness.

The dash and steering wheel are left as standard, but the normal front seats are replaced by two very special German-built Recaro seats which match the space-age concept of the interior. These high-backed rally-style seats have push buttons in the arms which control the position of the back and head-rest and pneumatically inflate three air bags in the squab panel to give precise lumbar support to any individual. The seat incorporates a heated centre section, which is also controlled from the panel in the arm-rest. The head-rests are fitted with stereo speakers connected to a stereo receiver/tape player, mounted in the dash.

Some interesting features of the Wolfrace Customs interior include two digital thermometers, three built-in calculators, two digital clocks and a mini computer, which works out average speed and estimated time of arrival. A futuristic glass fibre column houses a television, which can be remotely rotated from the rear seats, as well as a concealed drinks cabinet.

The interior is fully trimmed in tastefully blending Dralon material, while the floor is covered in thick pile carpet.

Cruising van appeals to couples

The appeal of the cruising van is very wide and easy to understand when considered in the context of the only real alternatives of the motor caravan proper and the car and trailer caravan. Caravans and motor caravans are ideal for a family with young children because holidays taken in them over a number of years are relatively cheap, and the almost prohibitive cost of eating out is saved by cooking 'at home'.

However, for couples without children the additional cost of eating out is much less, and the extra expense of the cooker, fridge and washing-up facility, not to mention the work involved, could easily carry the argument against cooking one's own food.

In the converted motor caravan too, the design of the seat is often compromised by the fact that it is expected to double as a bed and its comfort for touring is reduced as a result. The external appearance also tends to be functional rather than eye-catching.

Without these drawbacks though, a big roomy van still fulfills the need for mobile accommodation for singles and couples. Add a little sophistication, comfort, insulation from noise and temperature variations and an individualistic exterior look, and you arrive at the cruising van.

The dash panel and steering wheel are standard. Warm carpet in a sensible colour swathes the floor. In the arm-rests, the push-button controls for seat adjustment can be seen.

Note how the black paint below fender level increases the apparent ground clearance, yet provides a sleeker appearance.

A typical cruising van can provide personalised transport in armchair comfort with a high standard of insulation; sufficient kitchen equipment for a continental breakfast or picnic lunch or beach party; a very comfortable double bed up to 4 ft. 6-ins. wide; ample storage space, including a wardrobe and roof-rack; entertainment with a balanced four-speaker stereo radio/cassette player, and a sophisticated atmosphere with dimmer switch lighting control; sumptuous furnishings and wall to wall shag pile carpeting.

In America, Canada and Australia where cruising vans are well-established, the market divides into three categories:
1—the young, in their 20–30s, seeking independence and freedom,
2—the middle-aged whose families have grown up and left home, and
3—business users looking for a mobile office/accommodation, a leisure hire vehicle, or a promotional/publicity vehicle.

The floor has been insulated and the flooring panel laid. Always lay the floor panel before panelling the walls, to ensure that any condensation that forms on the walls will stay above the floor panelling, where it can be dealt with, instead of creeping below the floor where mildew could result. Insulation is 3-in. thick fibreglass. If you use this material, wear gloves and a mask, to avoid irritation by particles that float from it.

With floor panels and insulation in place, the seats can be positioned and their size checked.

Here the ceiling panel is in place and the construction of the seats can be plainly seen. Any seat for use in vehicles must be strongly built to withstand the vibrations set up by constant travel. Joints, although they can be simple, must be strong.

The fabulous Recaro seats—specially imported from Germany. They have fully adjustable backs, with inflatable lumbar supports and heated centre sections ... simply out of this world.

What a difference the final upholstery makes! Seats just made to be sat in! The orange glass fibre column houses the TV, which can be rotated by remote control from the rear seats. The column also conceals a drinks cabinet.

WOW! — Beautiful paintwork and finish on this American beauty caught by the camera of Ed. Monaghan.

Before indulging yourself in this orgy of technicolour paintwork, consider the consequences of even a minor skirmish with another vehicle—you might just decide on a plainer and more easily replaced finish on some of the more vulnerable areas.

A warm and comfortable interior. The U-shaped
bed covered in deep buttoned dralon has plenty of
storage space beneath.

More Custom
Goodies

A ladder makes loading and unloading easy, but remember that van roofs were not intended to support weight concentrated in one spot, so unless you have feet 3 ft. wide, don't stand on it!

Roof-racks

A roof-rack will give you the chance to use some of that valuable space above the van. Use the space for tents and other light-weight bulky items. Do not put heavy objects up there, as too much weight will make the van top-heavy, and affects its stability and handling. Make sure that anything that you do put on the rack is securely fixed.

Customized steering wheel

Racing-type steering wheels, besides adding another touch of elegance to the cab's interior, can also make the van more comfortable to drive. They are easy to fit as follows:

Turn the steering wheel so that the front wheels are straight ahead. The horn button usually unclips, so remove it. Remove the horn contact ring, exposing the column shaft of the steering wheel (and the centre retaining nut). Make a mark on the column shaft so that you know where the top position of the steering wheel is. Undo the centre retaining nut until it just comes over the top threads of the shaft. Fit the wheel puller in place and remove the steering wheel.

There should be an adapter with the custom steering wheel. Insert this adapter over the centre shaft of the steering column, making sure that the 'top' mark of the adapter lines up with the mark you made on the shaft. The horn wire will still be hanging loose, so insert it through its cover, and place the cover over the shaft. Put the custom steering wheel into place, and tighten up the small retaining bolts by hand (you just need to keep the steering wheel in the correct position while you put the large retaining nut on). Place this nut on the column shaft and tighten it fully, then remove the small retaining bolts. Place the horn ring over the shaft, replace the retaining bolts, and tighten them fully. Now connect the horn wire to its terminal on the horn ring. Fix the button spring to the horn button, and push both into the steering column. They should clip into place. Finally, test the horn, and you have finished.

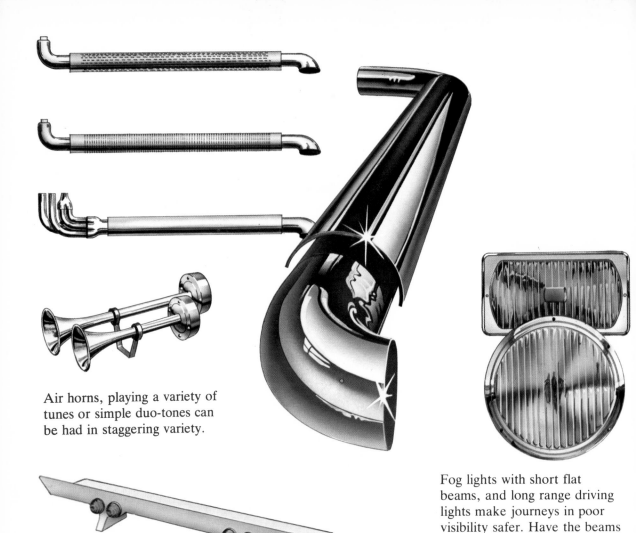

Air horns, playing a variety of
tunes or simple duo-tones can
be had in staggering variety.

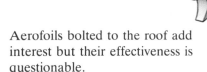

Aerofoils bolted to the roof add
interest but their effectiveness is
questionable.

Fog lights with short flat
beams, and long range driving
lights make journeys in poor
visibility safer. Have the beams
aligned by a garage.

Extra mirrors

Mirrors can often be replaced or modified to give
better rear vision (especially at night), or you can
change them to give a better appearance. You can
make existing mirrors look much more attractive
by simply painting them a matching or contrasting
colour to the van's scheme, or by replacing them by
more streamlined types. An interior mirror can be
replaced by an anti-dazzle mirror for more comfortable night vision, although most vans, due to
their height, are not affected by the lights of
following vehicles. Many owners have added small
murals to their wing mirrors to brighten them up,
but they are rather vulnerable to damage.

Exhaust and mufflers

Replacement exhaust pipes allow your engine to
breathe better, the side pipes may end in two, three
or four tubes.

They come in plain chrome, aluminium or matt
black, some with decorative lourvred or slotted
finish.

Dummies are also available, but are shunned by
the perfectionist.

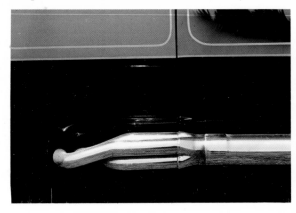

Three examples of 'Captain's Chairs'.
A simple change of seats can make a tremendous difference to the comfort of long distance driving. If you intend buying seats that swivel, ensure that your van model provides sufficient clearance in the cab.

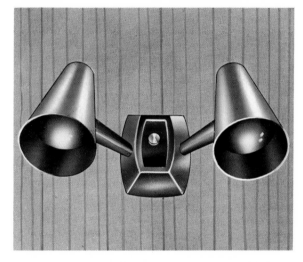

Good lighting is essential for reading—this type of light is ideal.

Tables with provision for holding glasses (and cups of course) are great for drinks underway, but don't drink and drive!

Seats

Standard seats can be quickly and simply exchanged for high back seats or Captains' chairs (high back chairs with armrests). Some of the better examples swivel and recline. The swivelling kind can also be used for sitting at the dining table, if this is correctly positioned.

Some motor caravans have front seats which are fully reclining, for night-time use. Having two longitudinal beds makes it unlikely that you will be able to fit a transverse double bed, so decide which you would prefer.

Most vanners opt for two side-facing settees that convert into a double bed, but week-enders may prefer the convenience of a fixed double at the rear which will preclude the fitting of other items, but is readily available when the fancy takes you.

Four tubes are the only outward
sign of a converted exhaust
system on this custom.

Just a few of the varied wheel types available.

Custom wheels

The true custom wheel is completely different from
the standard item. Mostly they are chrome-plated,
made in small numbers and are consequently
expensive. Most vanners opt for wide wheels with a
low profile and purchase their tyres at the same
time. The low profile, lowers the overall height of
the van, giving an appearance of increased
sleekness. When coupled with horizontal striped
paintwork, the apparent length is also increased.

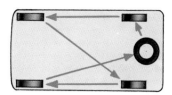
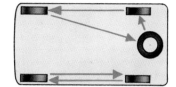

A typical cross-ply tyre.   A radial tyre.

Tyres

1. **Too low**—the tyre will overheat; the sides of the tread will wear quickly and the tyre plies will tend to separate.

2. **Too high**—riding comfort will be reduced, and the tyre will suffer from excessive wear in the centre of the tread and vulnerability to knocks.

3. **Correct**—the tyre gives optimum performance, the tread works over its entire width, thus ensuring uniform tyre wear and long life.

Changing over—to ensure even and uniform tyre wear and long tyre life, front and rear wheels and the spare should be changed over regularly, as shown in the diagram.

Balancing—whenever a tyre is changed, the wheel must be rebalanced. It should be remembered that unbalanced wheels cause unstable steering, abnormal steering gear and uneven tyre wear.

If you fit aluminium wheels to your van, remember that they are easily pitted by road salt. After snowy weather, when roads have been treated with salt, wash thoroughly with water and protect with a silicone wax polish.

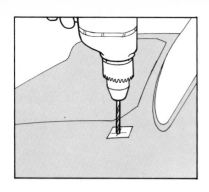  

Fitting an aerial

1. Decide on the best position and ensure that you can reach the underside, and that there is sufficient depth to accommodate any below-body part of the aerial.

2. Use a tank cutter, either by hand as shown, or as a drill attachment.

3. A typical aerial retaining assembly.

Console

If you want to add meters, clock, and switches for extra lights, you can have all the instruments and switches dotted around your dashboard, or you can gather them together on a console. Consoles can either be overhead, or they can be located between the driver's and passenger's seats—both types look impressive. There are some very good kits for overhead consoles on the market, most of which have room for a radio, and tape player, as well as space for all the switches and meters that you will need to install. Speakers can often go on the underside of the console, where they have the advantage of needing only short wires; routing wires from the front to the back of the van is a nuisance.

Hi-fi equipment

Speakers for a radio or cassette player usually go on either side of the van, at the rear, but you can fit them in the side doors if that will be easier. Install the wiring (both for stereos, and for any additional lights that you want to add to the interior of the van) before you panel. A radio will also need an aerial, so you will probably have to mount this and run the aerial lead as well, before panelling or head-lining is attached.

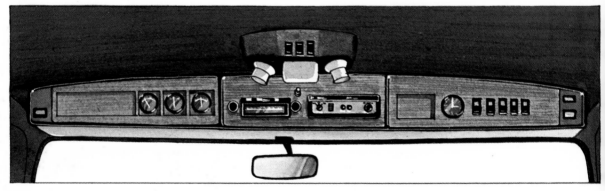

Installing a radio

If you decide to fit your own radio, you must take time to read the instructions carefully before proceeding. Most radios are simple to fit, providing you follow a set procedure.

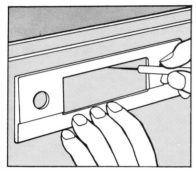

1. The manufacturer usually provides a template for cutting the slot and holes. Scribe and mark carefully.

2. Drill the holes.

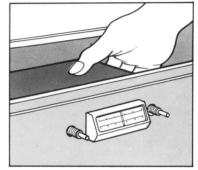

3. Fit the radio from the rear.

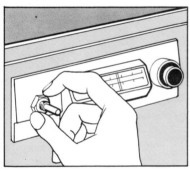

4. Attach the face-plate and the holding nuts.

5. Mark speaker positions, taking account of any flanges, lips or screw holes.

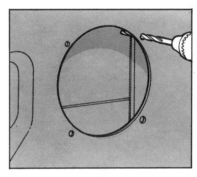

6. Drill the holes carefully.

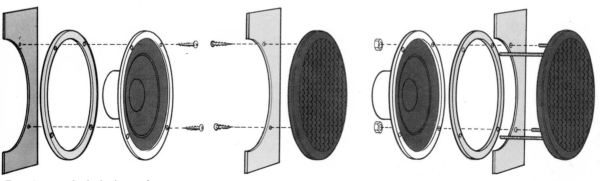

7. An exploded view of a typical speaker assembly.

Choosing a stereo system

When deciding which type of stereo you will have in your van, you will not be hampered by lack of choice. With many more people adding radios and cassette players to their cars and vans, manufacturers have risen to the occasion, and there is now an almost bewildering range of stereo and mono equipment on the market, all of which has been designed specially for use in vehicles. Should you buy a good quality expensive radio or cassette, or a not-so-good cheaper model? Cheap radios do not, in general, sound as good as more expensive ones, and are often harder to suppress. (One of the greatest problems of van radios is suppression. If you do not suppress the radio adequately, you will often get an irritating click when you switch the ignition on, and a lot of extra interference when you are moving. This can be so bad that you cannot hear the radio programme at all). Despite this, there are some good radios around, so listen to and compare as many sets as you can.

If you van is well furnished, panelled, and sound insulated, it might be worth getting a good radio, as you will probably be able to hear the difference between a good one and a cheaper model. Note that I say 'probably', the same radio will sound different in different vans, and it is very much a matter of personal preference. One thing is certain, if the wind whistles through a hole in the floor-boards, and the engine makes enough noise to make conversation difficult, then it won't be much use buying a good quality radio or cassette player.

If you will be driving near cities for most of the time, where there will usually be an FM transmitter, then it will be worth getting an FM radio (the quality of reception is better than an AM receiver). If you will be driving in hilly areas away from cities, then get an AM set (they are cheaper). If you buy an FM radio, make sure that it has interference-suppression circuitry.

You could experience trouble with interference on your radio and you may also need specialist advice on which model to buy, so purchase from a recognized dealer. It will also be wise to let him install it for you, as it will cost only a few pounds, and could save you a lot of trouble in the long run, especially if you have a combination of van and radio which is particularly difficult to suppress.

Eight-track cartridges are simple and reliable, but are becoming less popular because they are not compatible with other hi-fi systems (there are other reasons for them going out of favour, but that is the main one). They have an endless loop of tape which passes in front of the playback heads, so you can leave the tape playing continually if you want. Unfortunately, when the tape changes from one track to the other (about once every fifteen minutes), the piece of music you are listening to hasn't always finished, and so there is then an irritating silence for a few seconds until the music continues.

Cassettes do not have either of these problems, but you have to change the tape every half hour or so. If you do get a cassette player, ensure that you install it within easy reach of the driving seat. Some better quality machines have an auto-reverse mechanism which will automatically play the other side when the first side has finished. Both cassette and cartridge recorders have an advantage over radios—they do not suffer from interference.

You can buy a radio and cassette player combined into one unit, or you can buy them separately. If you want both, it will be worth buying them as one unit, as most combinations are small enough to fit into a standard dash-board aperture.

You should get good quality speakers to play your tape or radio through. An expensive radio or cassette will sound positively average through cheap speakers. The area behind the speakers should be enclosed, or their base response will be poor, and they will sound 'tinny'. For this reason, mounting directly onto the dash-board is not recommended.

Aerials for radio sets also vary tremendously in quality, although you can buy good ones which are quite inexpensive. You will be able to hear the difference, so buy a good one, and take professional advice. Telescopic stainless steel aerials are the most popular, as they are practical and give good reception.

Although it is better to get an expert to fit your radio, you may still decide to fit it yourself, and there are plenty of people who are able to do it as well as the expert, although it may take them longer.

Surprising how a custom paint job can increase the pride of ownership. Customized vans could be an investment for commercial users if more careful driving and valeting resulted from their use.

Fridges

Fridges must be installed properly to work well. Unless there is a good flow of air past the heat-exchanger (the coils at the back of the unit, and the fins at the top) the fridge will not work efficiently. Its base must also be horizontal to within a couple of degrees.

When you fit the fridge, to ensure that there will be enough air flowing round the back, you must provide at least one vent in the wall of the van behind the fridge. With a single inlet in the van wall, the warm air generated will pass into the van—not too comfortable on a hot day, when the fridge has to work its hardest, and thus produces the most heat. With a second vent installed, the warm air from the fridge can be expelled outside the van.

If you don't want to go to the trouble of installing a fridge, or live where it doesn't get hot enough to merit one, then it may be worth considering a cool-box. Cool-boxes work by evaporating the water that you add to them, and must be kept topped up. They are fine for keeping cold water, milk, and so on, but are heavy. Alternative light-weight cool-boxes make use of ice pack pre-frozen in an icebox and are fine for storing food for short periods of up to eight hours, but then require their packs to be refrozen.

A capacious water tank with triple outlet pipes. If sufficient space is available and an outside filler can be provided, solid tanks are fine. Otherwise plastic or rubber tanks take up less room and are easier to fill.

Simpler than a fridge, and good for picnic and fishing trips is this insulated ice box. Packs of pre-frozen coolant keep the temperature down for a few hours.

All the comforts of home with a mini fridge. Available from custom accessory shops and marine equipment dealers.

74

A catalytic heater.

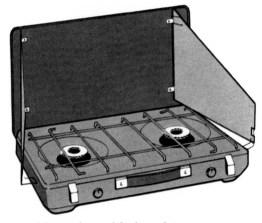

A portable cooker with draught protector flaps.

If you use a cooker inside the van an extractor hood will minimize the condensation problem.

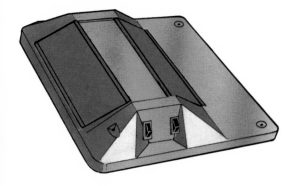

Heating

Even in a well-insulated van it can get cold and you will need some kind of heater. Unless you will be vanning in winter, a small one should be quite sufficient.

If you use a portable, unflued heater, you must ensure that you have plenty of ventilation in the van whenever the heater is working. Keep a couple of windows open, and never leave the heater on all night. Permanent vents are essential, but by themselves may be insufficient for extended use of the heater.

A better type of gas heater is one fitted with a flue; the air is drawn in from outside the van, and the waste products are expelled outside. Sometimes you can see the gas flame, but when you can, it is usually behind a glass cover: with this type of heater all that goes inside the van is the heat.

Catalytic heaters do not need flues, since they do not actually burn. You must first of all light them to get the action started, but then they will heat your van cheaply, cleanly and safely—without a flame. Although very safe, metal sheets should still be fixed to protect the back wall.

This is a luxury most vanners will go without, but a cooker with oven is useful for heating up take-away food and for a quick cook up on out-of-the-way sites.

Storage

Don't fit the cooker, sink unit, extra battery, beds and fridge all along the same side of the van—it will play havoc with the van's suspension (and the van will tilt so much that the fridge won't work anyway). Aim to distribute the load as evenly as possible when you are designing the interior lay-out of the van.

Cupboards are preferable to shelves, but if you have any shelves make sure that they have retaining lips on the edges. You should be able to open hinged cupboard doors with one hand, and sliding doors should not stick. Wardrobes can either be full or half length, but must be wide enough to hold a hanger full of clothes, hung face out from the wall. A roof-rack is ideal for transporting tents and camping beds, or any other bulky items, such as surf-boards and bicycles.

A portable flushing toilet with detachable holding tank beneath.

Toilet

Some kind of toilet facility in your van is very often welcome in an emergency or at night.

The simplest toilet is the bucket-type, which consists of a plastic bucket with a detachable toilet seat and a lid that fits tightly over the bucket rim to avoid spillages. The waste is sterilised and deodorised by adding chemicals, and it can be emptied at special disposal points provided at campsites.

Another type has a second compartment underneath the first, into which the contents of the first chamber are flushed and sterilised. The container is then emptied when convenient.

A third type is the recirculating toilet. This does not use fresh water each time it is flushed: when the toilet is flushed, the water is sterilised, filtered, and then recirculated by a pump, powered by the van's battery, to provide the next flush. The whole unit weighs less than an equivalent non-recirculating type, as it does not need such a large store of water.

Unless you don't mind the smell of deodorising liquid, then get a toilet with a flush, and make sure that the second chamber is hermetically sealed (it usually is).

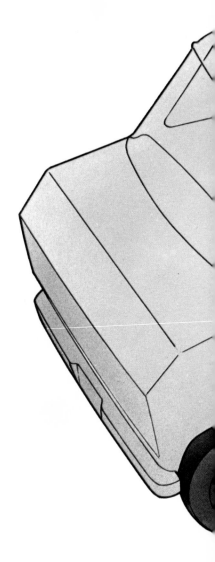

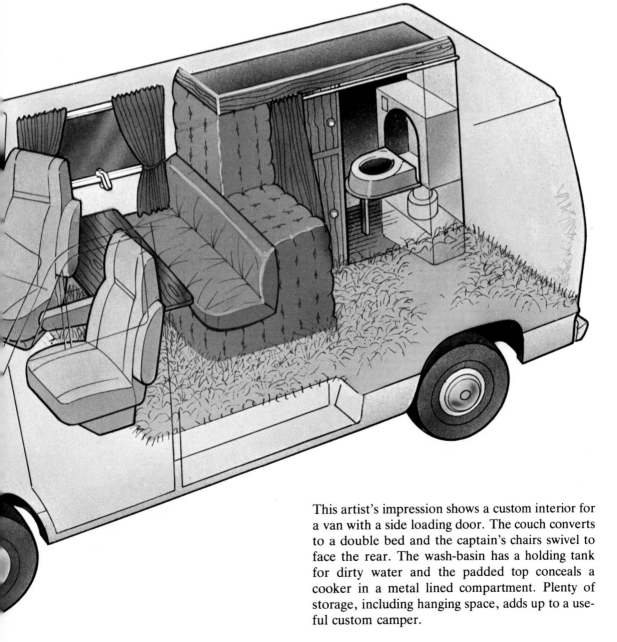

This artist's impression shows a custom interior for a van with a side loading door. The couch converts to a double bed and the captain's chairs swivel to face the rear. The wash-basin has a holding tank for dirty water and the padded top conceals a cooker in a metal lined compartment. Plenty of storage, including hanging space, adds up to a useful custom camper.

If you use a cooker inside the van an extractor hood will keep the condensation problem to a minimum.

If you must have everything, a steel sink and drainer, plus a water heater, are useful extras.

Curtained storage areas, divided into large shelved sections, are good for bulky items like blankets and sleeping bags.

This converted interior shows an ideal storage arrangement and space for fridge and cooker. Somewhere between caravan and custom there must be a suitable compromise.

While the average custom van fan will not want
to build a motor caravan, a great deal can be
learned and adapted from caravan conversions.
For vacations and long weekends it is surprising
the amount of gear that needs to be stowed so
storage is essential.
This example of a caravan conversion shows
optimum use of space.

Appendix

AER Developments,
Qua Fen Common, Soham, Cambs.
(Elevating Roof Kits)

AMS Trading (Amstrad) Ltd.,
89 Ridley Road, Dalston, London, E8.
(Car Stereos)

A 'n' D Custom,
162 Byron Avenue, Manor Park, London, El2.
(Spoilers)

A & L Autos,
96 North Street, Romford, Essex.
(Custom Paint Supplies)

Alexander Engineering Co. Ltd.,
Haddenham, Aylesbury, Bucks. HP17 8BZ.
(Accessories, including Steering Wheels)

American Auto Spares,
91 Moyser Road, Streatham, London, SW16.
(Wheels, Exhausts, etc.)

American Tyre Sales,
31/33 Fortune Green Road, London, NW6.

Americar,
352/354 Southchurch Road, Southend-on-Sea,
Essex.
(Tyres, Wheels, Accessories)

Autocar Electrical Equipment Co. Ltd.,
Chantry Road Industrial Estate, Kempston,
Beds. MK42 7SD.
(Car Stereos)

Auto Radio Services,
230 Hamilton Road, Motherwell, Scotland.
(Car Stereos)

John Brown Wheels,
226 Kilburn High Road, Kilburn, London, NW6.
(Front & Rear Spoilers, Fire Extinguishers,
Custom Stripes, etc.)
also at:
Wedgenock Lane, Wedgenock Industrial Estate,
Warwick.

226/232 London Road, West Croydon, Surrey.

35 Brislington Hill, Brislington, Bristol.

University Precinct Centre, Oxford Road,
Manchester.

Speedway Modern Service Station, Anwick
Corner, Sleaford, Lincs.

Brown & Geeson Ltd.,
1/23 Queens Road West, London, E13 OPA.

S. W. Brown & Co.,
Poole House, Farm Works, Alcester Road,
Portway, Birmingham.
(Elevating Roofs, etc.)

Budget Racing,
York Road, Ilford, Essex.

Cal Brook Cars,
Commerce Estate, Kingston Road, Leatherhead,
Surrey.
(Custom Paint Supplies)

Cambridge Coachworks,
45 Cambridge Road, Kingston, Surrey.
(Murals)

Car Camper Sales Co.,
6 Langmead, Westleigh Village, Instow,
N.Devon, EX39 4NP.
(Furniture Kits, Sliding & Louvre Windows,
Elevating Roofs, etc.)

The Car Radio Station,
45 Lordship Lane, East Dulwich, London, SE22.
(Car Stereos)

Caravan Accessories (Kenilworth) Ltd.,
10 Princes Drive, Kenilworth, Warks. CV8 2FD.
(Underfloor Tanks, Waste Water Tanks, etc.)

Cavendish Sales,
279/283 Whitechapel Road, London, E1.
(Stereo & Cassette Equipment)

Cobra Automotive Products Ltd.,
Heslop, Halesfield 23, Telford.
(Wheels)

Conversion & Tuning Centre,
Unit 1130, 41 Norwood Road, London, SE24.
also at:
45a Tulse Hill, London, SW2.

Coopers Seats & Windows Ltd.,
The Old Tannery, Station Road, Otley,
West Yorks.
(Panel Cutters Loaned, Head-Lining, Motor
Caravan Plans, etc.)

Creech Coach Trimming Centre,
67 High Street, South Norwood, London,
SE25 6EB.
(Interiors)

Deals-on-Wheels,
57 London Road, Romford, Essex.
also at:
977 London Road, Southend-on-Sea, Essex.
(Wide Wheels, Captain's Chairs, Airbrushes,
etc.)

Decca Radio & Television Ltd.,
Neachells Lane, Willenhall, Wolverhampton,
Staffs.
(Radio Equipment)

Exe Marine Ltd.,
Pound Place, Wolborough Street, Newton
Abbott, Devon.
(Custom Glassfibre)

Fesglade Ltd.,
18 Matthew Street, Dunstable, Beds.
(Intruder Alarms for Vans)

GJS Ltd.,
New Road, Pengam, Mid.Glamorgan,
South Wales, CF8 7XJ.
(Headlight Conversions, Captain's Chairs)

B. F. Goodrich,
257/259 Portland Road, South Norwood,
London, SE25.
(Mail Order only)
also at:
4 Bell Brook Estate, Uckfield, Sussex.

Whites Corner, London Road, Camberley,
Surrey.

114/116 Southampton Road, Salisbury, Wiltshire.

Valley Road, Plympton, Nr.Plymouth, Devon.

139 High Street, Honiton, Devon.

Marsh Barton Trading Estate, Grace Road,
Exeter, Devon.

Whitehall, Knighton, Powys.
(Tyres & Wheels)

Hitachi Sales (UK) Ltd.,
Hitachi House, Station Road, Hayes,
Middlesex, UB3 4DR.

Richard Holdsworth Conversions Ltd.,
Loddon Bridge Road, Woodley,
Nr. Reading, Berks. RG5 4BG.
(Motor Conversions, Furniture, Roof-Raising
Kits, etc.)

Howard-Lange Ltd.,
541 Brixton Station Road, London, SW9.
(Van Conversions)

Jeff Howe Exhausts,
Main Road (A20), West Kingsdown, Kent.
(Weber Parts, Wheels, Silencers, Lowering Kits,
etc.)

Lab-Craft Ltd.,
Church Road, Harold Wood, Romford, Essex.
(Electric Water Pumps, etc.)

Ladyline Outdoor Leisure Centre,
Royal Oak Centre, Brighton Road,
Purley, Surrey.
(Portable Toilets, Fridges, Catalytic Heaters,
Camping Accessories)

London Motorcaravans,
302/306 King Street, Hammersmith,
London, W6 9NH.
(Accessories, etc.)

Manchester Motorcaravan Co.,
3 Dulwich Street, Manchester, 4.
(High Tops, Furniture Kits, Accessories)

Mech-Spray,
11/16 Miles Place, Deluce Road,
Rochester, Kent.
(Custom Paint Supplies)

Motorola Automotive Products Division,
Taylors Road, Stotfold, Hitchin,
Herts, SG5 4AY
(Radio & Stereo Equipment)

National Panasonic (UK) Ltd.,
107/109 Whitby Road, Slough, Bucks, SL1 3DR.
(Stereo Equipment)

Thomas Ness Ltd.,
Coal House, Lyon Road, Harrow, Middx.
(Fresh-ness Water Filler & Purifier)

Westoop Ltd.,
St. Helens, Auckland, Bishop Auckland,
Co. Durham, DL14 9AA.
(Cooker Hoods with Extractor Fan)

Oxley Coachcraft,
Craven Street, Hull, Yorks.
(Motor Caravan Conversions)

Philips Electrical Ltd.,
420/430 London Road, Croydon,
Surrey, CR9 3QR.
(Stereo Equipment)

Pye Ltd.,
Car Radio Division, P.O. Box 49,
Cambridge, CB4 IDS.
(Stereo Equipment)

Quip Accessories,
Halifax Road, Dewsbury, W.Yorks.,
WF13 4AW.
(Distributors, Lamps, Spoilers, Shock Absorbers)

Radiomobile Ltd.,
Goodwood Works, North Circular Road,
London, NW2 7JS.
(Stereo Equipment)

Ripspeed International,
7 Pinner Green, Uxbridge Road, Pinner, Middx.
(Accessories)

Road & Racing Equipment,
135 Uxbridge Road, Hanwell, London, W7 3HH.
(Seats, Wheels, Steering Wheels)

Sextons (Stereo & Radio Equipment),
23 York Road, Waterloo, London, SE1.
also at:
180 Grays Inn Road, London, WC1.

37 Bedford Place, Southampton, Hampshire.

Shadow Marketing Services,
49 Watlington Street, Reading, Berks.
(Tyres & Wheels)

Simba,
Security House, Occupation Road, Walworth,
London, SE17.
(Car Alarms, Security Systems)

A. G. Thorpe (Development),
60 Wellington Street, Derby.
(Body Custom Kits)

The Van Shop GB,
341/5 Roman Road, London, E3.
(All Accessories)

Warwick & Bailey Ltd.,
Rockcliffe Works, Paterson Street,
Blackburn, BB2 3SP
(Elevating Roof Kits)

Weare Accessories,
306 Topsham Road, Exeter, Devon.
(Spoilers, Wide Wheels, Shock Absorbers, etc.)

Wolfrace Equipment,
Elms Industrial Estate, Shuttleworth Road,
Goldington, Bedford.
(Head Office & Mail Order)
also at:
3 Staples Corner, North Circular Road,
Edgware Road, London, NW2.
(Retail Shop—all Custom Accessories)

Wheels,
40/44 Western Avenue, Acton, London, N3.

Whitehall Conversions,
Globe Works, Whitehall Lane, Grays, Essex.
(Fixed & Elevating Roofs)

Appendix

A & R Truckin' Accessories, Inc.,
120 East Seneca Turnpike, Syracuse, New York.

Alphabet's Custom West,
821 W.Gardena Blvd., Gardena,
California 90247.

American Cycle & Van Works,
Route 35 & Vineyard Avenue, Morgan,
New Jersey.

Ametron Electronics,
1200 North Vine, Hollywood, California 90038.

Ancra Accessories,
133 Center Street, El Segundo, California 90245.

Armour Security,
1030 North Grove Street, Anaheim,
California 92806.

Art 'N' Fiberglass,
2016 Hammer Avenue, Norco, California 91760.

Auto World, Inc.,
701 N.Keyser Avenue, Scranton,
Pennsylvania 18508.

Avan Accessories,
214 Beechmont, Keego Harbor, Michigan.

Amon Book,
P.O. Box 8, Rochester, Michigan.

Auto-Haus,
P.O. Box 428, Buena Park, California 90621.

Avi Naftel, Avi's Custom Creations,
160 North Baldwin Street, Johnson City,
New York.

Big Red Auto Parts,
531 North College Avenue, Bloomington,
Indiana.

Bits & Pieces,
3201 Telegraph Avenue, Oakland, California.

Bolder Designs,
16131 Gothard Street (E), Huntington Beach,
California 92647.

Bon-Aire Industries,
3240 Industry Drive, Signal Hill,
California 90801.

Buckeye Cycle & Van Supply,
7626 Mentor Avenue, Mentor, North Carolina.

Buckeye Trick Trucks,
35 West Main, Dalton, Ohio.

Bumbarger's TV/RV.,
109 East Market Street, Cleafield, Pennsylvania.

Burmester Supply Co.,
2220 Scott Lake Road, Pontiac, Michigan.

Butterscotch Enterprises,
1172 Old Ralston Road, Rockford, Illinois.

California Van Art,
245 E.La Habra Blvd., La Habra,
California 90631.

J. Calloway's Van Specialities,
109 Greenbank Road, Greenbank Shopping
Center, Wilmington, California.

Carpetbagger,
1100 Pioneer Way, El Cajon, California 92020.

Cezon Cameo Parts,
13555 Valley Vista, Sherman Oaks,
California 91423.

Challenger Equipment Co.,
918 W.Foothill Blvd., Azusa, California 91702.

Chicagoland Van Centre,
7227 West Roosevelt Road, Forest Park, Illinois.

Coleman Bros. Speed Shop,
7443 Washington Blvd., Baltimore, Maryland.

Color Man,
1713 N.Orange Thorpe Park, Anaheim,
California 92801.

The Crazy Painters,
9665 Alondra Blvd., Bellflower, California 90706.

Crows Custom Aquarium & Van Supplies,
212 West Milwaukee Street, Jefferson,
Wisconsin.

D & A Four Way,
1090 Guilderland Avenue, Hartsdale, New York.

Dan Woods Ent.,
15516 Vermont Avenue, Paramount,
California 90723.

Darrell's Custom Van & Auto Trim,
Route 2, Box 424, Manhattan, Kansas.

Deluxe Trailer Supply,
8595 Rosecrans, Paramount, California.

Desert Dynamics,
13720 E.Rosecrans, Santa Fe Springs,
California 90670.

Dick Cepek,
9201 California Avenue, South Gate,
California 90280.

Discount Van Decor, Inc.,
728 Bel Air Road, Unit 110 & 111, Bel Air,
Maryland.

DOBI (Dept. M),
P.O. Box 5071, Santa Monica, California 90405.

E & G Classics, Inc.,
4419 Baltimore Avenue,
Bladensburg, Maryland.

Edjans Custom Van Accessories,
G-5418, S.Dort Hwy., Flint, Michigan.

Fancy Vans & Speed,
Route 7, Box 155A, Waldorf, Maryland.

Far-Go Custom Vans & Cars,
2323 East 8 Mile Road, Warren, Massachusetts.

Far Performance, Inc.,
1931 Old Middlefield Way, Mountain View,
California 94040.

Fleming Urethane Prod.,
1045-A West Collins Avenue, Orange,
California 92667.

Flite-Tronics Company,
2221 Empire Street, Burbank, California 91504.

Garden State Van Conv., Inc.,
1044 Main Avenue, Clifton, New Jersey.

Genuine Suspension,
1361 E.Pomona, Santa Ana, California 92705.

Gila River Products,
105 South 43rd Street, Phoenix, Arizona 85034.

Goober's Van Accessories,
7157 Greenwell Springs Road, Baton Rouge,
Louisiana.

Good Times, Inc.,
3500 Pioneer Pkwy. West, Arlington,
Texas 6013.

Graham Enterprises,
9618 S.Santa Fe Springs Road, Santa Fe Springs,
California 90670.

Gratiot Auto Supply,
Box 870-B10-Royal Oak, Michigan 48086.
(Accessories)

Harry Morrow Autobooks,
2900 West Magnolia Blvd., Burbank, California.

Hayward Recreational Center,
24895 Mission Blvd., Hayward, California.

Hickey Enterprises,
1645 Callens Road, Ventura, California 93003.

Hi Enterprises,
11709 Cardinal Circle, Garden Grove,
California 92643.

Hi Rev,
215 East 29th Street, Marshfield, Wisconsin.

also at:
413 Galloway, Eau Claire, Wisconsin.
508 Monroe Street, Green Bay, Wisconsin.
536 North Grand Avenue, Schofield, Wisconsin.

H C Hilites,
P.O. Box 155, Williams, Arizona 86046.

Holiday Wheels,
7200 Acacia Avenue, Garden Grove,
California 92641.

Holley Carburetor Division,
Colt Industries, P.O. Box 749, Warren,
Michigan 48090.
(Fuel Pumps, etc.)

Hooker Headers,
1032 W.Brooks Street, Ontario, California 91762.

House of Stewart,
16123 Runnymede Street, Van Nuys,
California 91405.

Imaginary Glass,
5419 E.La Palma, Anaheim, California 92807.

Joe Bailon,
5955 Troost Avenue, N.Hollywood,
California 91607.

Kamp, Inc.,
1745 W.134th Street, Gardena, California 90249.

Karvan International,
1401 S.Village Way, Santa Ana,
California 92705.

King's Kustom Koaches,
172/174 West Winghocking Street, Philadelphia,
Pennsylvania.

Louisiana Custom Vans,
180 North Cities Service Hwy., Sulphur,
Louisiana.

Low Manufacturing,
245 W.Foothill Blvd., Monrovia,
California 91016.

Mag Buff,
3008 S.Orange, Santa Ana, California 92707.

Magic Ryhtm Caravans, Inc.,
5710 West 79th Street, Burbank, California.

Martin Enterprises,
P.O. Box 882,
Marina Del Rey, California 90291.

Marty's Upholstery & Custom Vans,
183 S.Kinzie, Bradley, Illinois.

Meguiar's Mirror Bright,
P.O. Box 17177, Irvine, California 92713.

M G Mitten, Inc.,
44 S.Chester Avenue, Pasadena,
California 91106.

Motorette Corp.,
6014 Reseda Blvd., Tarzana, California 91356.

Mothers Mag Polish,
1950 Newport Blvd., Costa Mesa,
California 92627.

Motion Performance Parts, Inc.,
598 Sunrise Highway, Baldwin, L.I.,
New York 11510.
(All Custom Accessories, Export Specialists)

Nationwise Rod Shop,
P.O. Box 27168, Columbus, Ohio 43227.
(Steering Wheels & Other Accessories)

Ohio Valley Van Parts,
5 North Second Street, Tipp City, Ohio.

Old Glory Vans,
11628 Artesia Blvd., Artesia, California 90701.

Pk's Motor Sales,
1774 Elida Road, Lima, North Carolina.

Pace-Setter, Inc.,
3455 S.La Cienega, Los Angeles,
California 90016.

Page-Alert Security,
23840 Madison Street, Torrance,
California 90505.

Pacer Performance,
5345 San Fernando Road West, Los Angeles,
California 90039.

Peninsula Truckin Co.,
670 El Camino Real, Redwood City, California.

Performance Vans,
261 Central Avenue, Hartsdale, New York.

Poorman's R.V. Center,
4½ Neptune, Morgan City, Louisiana.

R & E Vans,
2313 Jackson Street N.E., Minneapolis,
Minnesota.

Recmar Plastics,
18111 Mt. Washington, Fountain Valley,
California 92708.

Recreational Vans, Inc.,
24747 Crenshaw Blvd., Torrance,
California 90505.

Ron's Van Plan,
Va Avenue, Hwy. 220, Collinsville, Virginia.

Roselle Custom Coach,
25th South Park Street, Roselle, Illinois.

Royce Electronics Corp.,
1746 Levee Road, North Kansas City,
Missouri 64116.

Safety Step,
1328 E.Edinger, Santa Ana, California 92705.

Salem Off-Road Center,
2715 Portland Road N.E., Salem, Oregon.

Secure-It,
Armour Security,
1030 North Grove Street, Anaheim,
California 92806.

Select Vans, Inc.,
606 W. Katella Avenue, Orange,
California 92667.

Sonday's Vans,
9230 120th Avenue, Kenosha, Wisconsin.

Spartan Plastics,
P.O. Box 67, Holt, Michigan 48842.

Steve's Paint'n Place,
17452 Clark Avenue, Bell Flower,
California 90706.

Street Customs Ltd.,
11737 Cardinal Circle, Garden Grove,
California 92643.

Stretch-Forming Corp.,
10870 Kalamar River Road, Fountain Valley,
California 92708.

Stull Industries,
7335 Orange Thorpe, Buena Park,
California 90621.

Sure Safe, S & S Research & Electronics,
6308 Woodman Avenue, Van Nuys,
California 91405.

T & H Vanworks Unlimited,
7833 Canoga Avenue, Canoga Park, California.

Taylor Made, Inc.,
5625 Kearny Villa Road, Sandiego, California.

Thee Iron Horse,
29 South 2nd Street, Fulton, New York.

The Truckin' Shop,
601 Lakeport Road, Chittenango, New York.

The Van House of Baltimore,
8816 Orchard Tree Lane, Towson, Maryland.

The Van House of Philadelphia,
Route 73 & Collins Avenue, Berlin, New Jersey.

The Van House of Richmond,
5717 Charles City Circle, Richmond, Virginia.

The Van Man,
2100 Arden Way, Sacramento, California.

The Van Shoppe,
10162-D Jefferson Avenue, Newport News,
Virginia.

Today's World Interiors,
3521 Tweedy Blvd., South Gate,
California 90820.

Traditional Coach Works,
9344 N.Oso Street, Chatsworth, California 91311.

Trimbrite,
P.O. Box 67, Holt, Michigan 48842.

Tri-Mil,
2740 S.Compton Avenue, Los Angeles,
California 90011.

Truck and Van Accessories,
1721 Poplar Avenue, Memphis, Tennessee.

Truck 'n Van Accessories,
1594 S.Anaheim Blvd., Anaheim,
California 92805.

Unipro (Van-Rac),
P.O. Box 4401, Burbank, California 91503.

Van Boogie,
2716 S.41st Street, Tacoma, Washington.

Van Designs, Inc.,
100 Windom Street, Allston, Massachusetts.

Van Man,
Lewis Road, Rogersford, Pennsylvania.

Van Parts Distribution,
92 South Case Avenue, Akron, Ohio.

Van-R-Us,
214 North Main, Almont, Michigan.

Van Shack, Inc.,
5916 S.W.Freeway, Houston, Texas.

Van Stuff, Inc.,
615 Route 23,
Pompton Plains, New Jersey.

Vanner 2 Van Center,
1021 West Dakota Street, Milwaukee, Wisconsin.

Vanners Inn,
3410 Altoona Avenue, Cleveland, Ohio.

Vans Ltd.,
379 South Street, Marlboro, Massachusetts.

Van'Tasia,
14523 South Hawthorne Blvd., Lawndale,
California.

Vantasia,
310 W.Aaron Drive, State College, Pennsylvania.

Van-Tastic, Inc.,
P.O. Box 4172, Inglewood, California 90309.

Vantasyland,
4410 Stamp Road, Marlow Heights, Maryland.

Vibra-Larm,
Adalarm Company,
432 North Tustin Avenue, Orange,
California 92667.

Vilem B. Haan, Inc.,
11401 W.Pico Blvd., Los Angeles,
California 90064.

Vulcan Custom Vans,
614 Woodward Road, Midfield, Alabama.

Wes Jerde Van Center,
11114 Hickman Mills Drive, Kansas City,
Missouri.

White's Van Alley,
P.O. Box 322,
16111 S.State, South Holland, Illinois.

Whitlock Performance Center,
10130 West Appleton Avenue, Milwaukee,
Wisconsin.

Wilcap Company,
2930 Sepulveda Blvd., Torrance,
California 90510.

140 Vans,
3152 Balto Blvd., Rt.140, Finksburg, Maryland.

4 x 4 & Van Center Ltd.,
967 Thayer Avenue, Silver Spring, Maryland.

Acknowledgements:

The publisher wishes to acknowledge the assistance of the following, who supplied photographs for this book.

Ed Monaghan Photographic,
3212 N.Main, Royal Oak, Michigan 48073, USA.

Andrew Morland,
Old Glade Cottage, Water Lane, Butleigh, Nr. Glastonbury, Somerset.

Colour reproduction: Kleur Litho, 6 Harcourt Rd., Bexleyheath, Kent

Artwork: Terry Allen Designs Ltd., St. Albans, Herts.

The National Street Van Association

The N.S.V.A. is really of international scope, with the original membership in the United States and associated divisions in Australia, Canada and the U.K. It was formed to cater for the enthusiast who enjoys not only van, but street machines, drag racing, cruising, and all the various aspects of the 'West Coast' automotive style. To support the growing craze of custom trucking in Britain, the N.S.V.A. strives to promote the friendly atmosphere of a national van club and encourages growth to a point when it may evolve to the primary function of co-ordinating the efforts of smaller local clubs.

It is surprising that the street van craze didn't start years ago in a big way, as the peculiarities of the U.K. weather seem to make the custom van a highly practical way to go. We would like to make it clear that street (custom) vans should not really be confused with standard commercially assembled campers, etc., although some of our members have used these as starting points for some really outstanding customizing. Insulation and sound-proofing materials can make a van as cosy as your own home and, since vanners cover many miles attending a great number of events each year, it makes sense to do it in comfort as well as style. Trucks offer virtually unlimited scope for custom paint designs and luxurious interiors. If you fancy drive train mods or engine swaps, they are ideal. Nearly all commercial vehicles have a proper chassis-frame that can be adapted to support most any engine configuration. You will usually find more space for mods of this type than in cars. There are a few vans in the U.K. with genuine mid-engine set-ups. A street van is invariably a 'one of a kind' modified to serve the owner's individual needs and finished to reflect his own personal taste. While it is entirely feasible to have a 'dual purpose' van, more often the result is a 'pleasure only' portable party rather than a mere goods vehicle.

The National Street Van Association invites you to join in the fun of freedom on wheels.

Keep on Truckin'

U.S.A. address:
89 Grant Street,
Crystal Lake,
Illinois 60014

U.K. address:
Home Farm Brunstead,
Stalham,
Norwich,
Norfolk.